The Way of the Cross for Teens

Walking with Jesus to Calvary

Therese Johnson Borchard

Pflaum Publishing Group
Dayton, OH

Cover and Interior Design: Kathryn Cole
Editor: Karen Cannizzo
Photos: W.P. Wittman Limited and
Copyright © istockphoto.com bobbieo

Fourth Printing: 2011

Pflaum Publishing Group
2621 Dryden Road, Suite 300
Dayton, OH 45439
800-543-4383
pflaum.com

ISBN 978-1-933178-37-0

The Stations

Introduction

he stations of the cross began as a way for Jesus' disciples to honor and remember their friend after his death. Believers wanted to walk the Way of Sorrows, the same steps that their Lord and Savior had walked. They wanted to return to important places associated with Jesus' life, death, and resurrection. This pilgrimage toward Calvary helped them recall, understand, and appreciate the greatest of Christian stories—the dying and rising of Christ Jesus.

The devotion or practice of the stations originated and developed from the need to remember and meditate on the sacred events that make up our Christian story of redemption, the paschal mystery. Just as the early disciples needed a way to remember and honor their Lord, we, too, gather to reflect on his suffering on our behalf, his generous offering of self for our salvation.

We take time during this devotion to think about what it means to be believers and followers of Christ and about the responsibility that comes with our faith. We remember and reflect on the words Jesus spoke to his disciples and what those words mean for us today.

> *"If any want to become my followers, let them deny themselves and take up their cross and follow me. For those who want to save their life will lose it, and those who lose their life for my sake will find it. For what will it profit them if they gain the whole world but forfeit their life? Or what will they give in return for their life?"*

Matthew 16:24

How to Use This Book

There are many ways to use this book. You can choose to:
• Use it on your own or with a group of your friends.
• Meditate on all the stations at one time. (This will probably take about an hour.)
• Spend a few minutes prayerfully reflecting on one station each day for a number of days.

However you choose to use this book, open yourself to the stations and what they tell us about Jesus' passion and death. Talk to Jesus. Tell him how you feel about what he has done for us. Challenge yourself to put lessons learned from the stations into action in your own life. If that seems too difficult, remember that after his death and resurrection, Jesus sent the Holy Spirit to guide us. Trust that the Holy Spirit will help you to lead a life inspired by Jesus' great love.

First Station

Jesus Is Condemned

hink about the moment when Pontius Pilate, Governor of Judea, condemns our Lord to die. Jesus, innocent of the crime with which he is charged, is handed over to Pilate by the chief priests, elders, and scribes because he is a threat to their authority and power.

In jealousy and envy, the Sanhedrin accuses Jesus of blasphemy and calls for Pilate to have him crucified, the worst punishment for any crime. Pilate, knowing in his heart that Jesus is innocent, tries to get out of sentencing Jesus to be crucified.

Because it is Passover, a most important feast for Jewish people, Pilate offers to release one prisoner. He is quick to suggest that they ask for the release of Jesus, the "King of the Jews" (Mark 15:9). Instead the people demand that Jesus be crucified, and another prisoner—a man named Barabbas—be freed.

Meditation

All of us come across situations in which we are forced to choose between what is right and what is wrong. It is difficult in these times to see things clearly. Often we are blinded by what other people want us to do. Our natural instinct is to try to please people, especially our friends.

If the elders and scribes had been able to see clearly, they would have realized that it was because of their jealousy—because they felt personally threatened by Jesus—that they condemned an innocent man to die. If Pilate had had the strength and integrity to do what was right, he would have followed his conscience and freed Jesus.

Jesus calls us to do the right thing. He knows what is in our hearts. The truth is there, among our other desires. Jesus asks us to search within ourselves, in our hearts and consciences, for the right decision. Then, when we identify the truth, he asks us to act justly.

Reflection

Think for a moment about a decision you are struggling to make. You may be confused, not knowing what's right. Or you may know what the truth is, but you want very much to ignore it. Maybe you feel threatened by someone at school who has joined your group of friends and has, in some ways, taken your place. Maybe your teacher has accused you of something you know you did, but you are tempted to deny your action to avoid the consequences. Gather these thoughts, fears, and questions in your heart, and reflect on them quietly.

Pause for silent reflection.

Prayer

We pray to Jesus, our Lord, who was unjustly condemned to die.

Lord, help me always try to do the right thing. Even when I am threatened by the truth, help me accept it, and grant me the strength to act with justice and compassion.

Second Station

Jesus Carries the Cross

hink about the moment when Jesus is handed his cross. He has done nothing to deserve crucifixion. He has only spoken the truth to those in power. And yet he is forced to carry an unbearable weight upon his shoulders. For a seemingly endless time, he must drag an awkward and heavy cross to the place where he will be crucified.

Jesus accepts his cross gracefully. He does not yell profanities at those who have unjustly condemned him. He does not shout for help. He humbly takes the weight of the cross upon his shoulders and begins to walk the road to Calvary.

Meditation

We all carry crosses of some kind. Some are heavy, like the grief over the death of a parent or other loved one. Some are easily seen, like a physical disability that makes us stand out from the rest of the crowd. Some are hidden deep within our hearts. In fact, few people, possibly no one at all, may know these burdens exist. We take the weight of all these kinds of crosses on our shoulders, and we carry them toward Calvary.

Jesus walks beside us on our Way of Sorrows. Having carried the heaviest cross of all—the weight of our sins—he journeys with us to Calvary. Knowing exactly what we hold in our hearts, he lightens our burden. He is there alongside us, lifting the weight from our shoulders.

Reflection

 Think for a moment about the cross that you are carrying. Perhaps you are struggling with a family problem, like the divorce of your parents. Or perhaps you are upset with a friend who has turned away from you.

Think about the crosses that people all around you carry. Some are crosses you know about—the problems and anxieties that friends, siblings, and parents have shared with you. But some are the crosses of persons you don't know—children suffering from hunger and disease in underdeveloped countries, abused wives hiding from their spouses, families displaced and separated by war, terrorism, and natural disasters. Think about the crosses that people carry today.

Pause for silent reflection.

Prayer

We pray to Jesus, our Lord, who carried the cross of our sins on his shoulders.

Lord, lighten the burden and weight of my cross. Grant me the strength and perseverance to carry my cross gracefully so that I might show others the consolation that comes in your name.

Third Station

Jesus Falls the First Time

Think about the moment when Jesus first falls. He is already humiliated in front of the crowd, dragging a massive cross over his shoulders as people shout at him and make fun of him. And then he falls. The heavy cross drops down on him, crushing what little strength he has left.

Think about the pain Jesus must have felt as the rough wooden cross scraped open sores caused by the scourging he endured just moments before. But he has no way to care for his wounds. He must gather all of his energy to lift the cross and start walking once more toward his death at Mount Calvary.

Meditation

How embarrassing it is to fall flat on our faces. At one time or another, all of us have fallen in some way. Maybe we have experienced a physical fall, like the fall of our Lord, where we literally have to pick ourselves up from the floor. Most often, however, we experience falls of another sort—when we feel as though we have failed miserably at something we have tried hard to attain or achieve. Perhaps we have failed at a sport or in class. Perhaps we feel we have failed in a social situation, either in or outside of school.

It is tempting to give up right there and then. We want to say, "Forget it! Enough!" and be done with it forever. But Jesus calls us to get up from the floor and try again. As we fell when we learned to walk, so we must fall at times throughout our lives to get to the places where we want to be.

Jesus is our support along the way. As we lie on the ground discouraged and disillusioned with ourselves, he is our helping hand, encouraging us to walk once more toward our goal.

Reflection

Think for a moment about something at which you feel you've failed. Maybe it is a physical goal—a marathon that you could not run because of an injury or ten pounds that you haven't been able to lose. Perhaps you've been unsuccessful at accomplishing a personal goal—to control your anger, to study more, or to stop smoking. Now take a moment to recommit yourself to your goal.

Pause for silent reflection.

Prayer

We pray to Jesus, our Lord, who fell many times on his way to be crucified for us.

Lord, lift me from my fall. Grant me the stamina and endurance to begin again the journey to my goal.

Fourth Station

Jesus Meets His Mother

hink about how difficult it must have been for Mary to see her son suffering on his way to Calvary. To have your son or daughter die before you is, perhaps, the worst tragedy to endure. But to see your son put to death for a crime that he did not commit—we cannot imagine Mary's confusion and sadness. This woman who carried the Messiah in her womb, gave birth to him, and raised him must have experienced her own crucifixion. And yet she stays composed. Her faith in God is strong. She trusts that her son's suffering is for the good, and that there will come a time when she will understand.

Meditation

Parenthood or guardianship—the responsibility of looking after and caring for another—is difficult.

Maybe over the course of your life you have had to care for a friend, neighbor, brother, or sister. Perhaps you have had to offer a friend or relative emotional support or lend that friend or relative some money. Maybe you've had to care for someone who is ill—making meals, running errands.

If you have experienced being a caregiver in any way, you have probably also experienced the pain of seeing someone you care for suffer. And you suffer with that person.

Reflection

Think about the person or people for whom you have cared, either physically—by preparing meals or changing diapers—or emotionally—by offering support or insight at a time of pain or confusion. Think about any time that you have suffered with and for someone you care for.

Now think about Mary and the pain she must have experienced at seeing her son suffer.

Pause for silent reflection.

Prayer

We pray to Mary, who suffered with her son.

Mary, you felt the pain and frustration of seeing your son suffer and die, and yet you trusted in the goodness of God. In your wisdom, teach us to love and trust as you did.

Fifth Station

Simon Helps Jesus

Think about the moment when Simon is forced to help Jesus carry the cross. Simon does not volunteer to help out of compassion for the suffering man. Simon is just passing by, a spectator to the events. He is ordered to lighten Jesus' burden so that Jesus would die as the Jewish leaders intended—crucified on the cross and not under the weight of the cross on the road to Calvary.

Meditation

From time to time all of us are given jobs that we don't enjoy or for which we didn't volunteer. We can't successfully avoid all of the bothersome tasks with which we are confronted.

However, we do have a choice about *how* we accept the job. We can gripe and complain about how unfair it is that we were assigned the task. Or we can accept the job with a positive attitude, thinking lovingly about the person whom we are helping. We can remain closed-minded, thinking only of ourselves and of our own schedules.

Or we can offer up a prayer for the person whom we may not know who is most likely going through a difficult time.

Jesus calls us to offer care and compassion to others, even when doing so may inconvenience us.

Reflection

Think for a moment about the last time you were unexpectedly called on to do a job for which you didn't volunteer. Maybe you found yourself helping someone with a flat tire alongside a busy highway. Or maybe you got stuck baby-sitting the neighbor's kids because of a family emergency. You wanted to be somewhere else, but there was no escaping the situation.

Next time you are asked to help out at the last minute, try to do the job with a positive attitude and offer up a prayer for the person in need.

Pause for silent reflection.

Prayer

We pray to Jesus, our Lord, who is always merciful, assisting us at all times and in all places.

Lord, help me to become more generous with my time. Direct me toward charity, and teach me patience. Assist me in works of love.

Sixth Station

Veronica Wipes Jesus' Face

Think about the courage of Veronica, coming forward to wipe the sweat and blood from Jesus' face. Aside from his mother, she is the first to show Jesus compassion along the Way of Sorrows. She tenderly embraces him, trying in her own small way to alleviate some of his suffering. Unlike Simon, who was forced to help Jesus, she voluntarily comforts our Lord, risking public humiliation and scorn.

As Jesus leaves her and begins walking once more toward death, this woman of faith is left with a beautiful imprint of his face on her veil, a precious gift given to her in return for her selfless act of love.

Meditation

All of us have been in situations where injustice is being done. We are uncomfortable because we know that what is happening is not right, but we are afraid to do or say anything.

When a person goes against the crowd, the crowd may turn against that person. The crowd could easily have started throwing things at Veronica, even demanding that she be punished. But she took that risk to wipe the sweat and blood from Jesus' face.

Jesus asks us to show the same integrity, courage, and compassion that Veronica did.

Reflection

How many times could a simple act of love have made a difference to someone we saw in pain? How many times have we wanted to step up and help but were afraid? How many times have we hidden our talents and gifts, our resources, so that we would not be asked to help?

Think about a person you know who could use your assistance. How can you help? What unique gifts can you offer?

Pause for silent reflection.

Prayer

We pray to Jesus, our Lord, who is there to wipe the sweat and blood from our faces.

Lord, lend me the strength and courage that I need to follow Veronica's example—to offer comfort and consolation to those who need it.

Seventh Station

Jesus Falls Again

Think about the moment when Jesus falls for a second time. The elders and scribes have already ordered Simon to help Jesus, hoping this will enable him to make it to the place of crucifixion. But he falls again.

He is so weak that the weight of the cross pushes him down. As he hits the ground a second time, the people throw objects at him, ridicule him, and shout things that hurt even more than the bleeding wounds on his body.

Meditation

It is much more difficult to pick ourselves up from a second fall than from a first. Our excuses for quitting are stronger. We have more reasons for giving up. And our determination to succeed is often lost.

When Jesus fell the second time, his pain intensified. Yet he stood up with courage, pulled the cross back onto his shoulders, and went along his way.

Jesus calls us to rise from each fall and to walk with him toward the place we wish to go. He doesn't promise an easy trip. In fact, he warns us of the difficulties of choosing the narrow and less traveled road. But he promises to accompany us on this road if we choose to walk it.

We learn from the Gospels that it is never too late to begin again. Even those who have made many wrong turns can find their way if they want to.

Reflection

Think about a goal for which you have virtually given up hope. Why do you think you are incapable of reaching that goal? Do you lack the confidence to pursue it because you have already failed once?

In this time, remember our Lord, who fell not once, but three times, on his way to Calvary. In his pain and suffering, Jesus pushed on, as we are called to do. Pray to him for the strength to lift yourself from a second fall and begin again.

Pause for silent reflection.

Prayer

We pray to Jesus, our Lord, who lifted himself from his falls to be crucified for us.

Lord, grant me the courage and determination to walk once more with you toward my destination.

Eighth Station

The Women Weep for Jesus

Think about the moment when Jesus sees the women of Jerusalem weeping for him. In all of his suffering and pain, how could he have noticed the sorrow of others? Yet, even in this darkest hour, he seeks to console and comfort his people. Jesus turns to the women and says, "Daughters of Jerusalem, do not weep for me, but weep for yourselves and for your children" (Luke 23:28).

With perfect compassion, he tells them to care for one another and for their children. He thinks not about himself, for he knows that his suffering needs to happen for the greater glory of God. His concern is for the people who hurt with him; and to those, he offers eternal consolation.

Meditation

We hate to see our friends suffer. Most of us have been there for friends struggling with problems at home or school. We feel their frustration and sense their pain. We want to take away their hurt, but we can't. We can only stay with them, watching them resolve the issue in their own time and in their own way.

The women who wept for Jesus along the road to Calvary could do only that—weep and feel his pain. Unable to carry his cross for him, they offered him their hearts.

As Jesus passed the women, he was touched by their sorrow. Their tears most likely brought brief relief to his suffering, or at least consolation in his pain.

We can do the same for our friends. Although we cannot solve their problems, we can offer comfort and companionship in times of loneliness and confusion.

Reflection

Think about someone you know who is struggling with a problem. Is it difficult for you to watch your friend experience the frustration and pain that is part of resolving the issue? Do you feel the urge to take away all of your friend's suffering or to somehow solve the problem yourself? It is very difficult just to sit with a person who is struggling, to be there as a friend and companion.

Pause for silent reflection.

Prayer

We pray to Jesus, our Lord, who hears our cries.

Lord, be with me when I am in trouble. Then teach me your mercy so I can ease the pain of others.

Ninth Station

Jesus Falls the Third Time

Think about the last time Jesus falls. By now he is no doubt completely exhausted and numbed by all the pain he is feeling. But he gets up—one final time—to make the last stretch to Calvary. How, in all of his suffering and torment, could he have found the strength to stand this last time, to lift the awkward and heavy cross, and to carry it once more on his shoulders?

Jesus' spirit remained strong, urging him on to the place of crucifixion so that all would be fulfilled as it was written in the Scriptures.

Meditation

By the time we have fallen the third time, many of us have given up hope completely. "Why should I go on?" we ask ourselves. "It is obvious that I will fail if I try again," we rationalize. Because the odds seem to be against us, we surrender.

Jesus tells us otherwise. Even in the face of impossible odds, he commands us to begin again, to start walking once more toward our goal.

If anyone had an excuse to quit, it was our Lord. Having already been scourged, mocked, and crowned with thorns, he carried an unbearable weight on his shoulders, falling three times. Yet he was determined to die according to God's plan for our salvation.

We are called to follow Jesus' example—to press on with determination toward our goal.

Reflection

Think about a mission that you have written off as impossible. Why have you given up on it? Is it because you have failed numerous times and you are convinced the pattern won't change?

Jesus tells us that we can accomplish anything if we have faith in him—that with God all things are possible. With God's help, we can succeed despite past failures.

Pause for silent reflection.

Prayer

We pray to Jesus, our Lord, who fell three times on the Way of Sorrows.

Lord, grant us the spirit of hope that inspired and encouraged you to lift yourself three times from the ground to complete your mission.

Tenth Station

Jesus Is Stripped

Think about the moment when Jesus reaches his destination, the place called Calvary, or *Golgatha,* "the place of a skull" (Mark 15:22). He has used up nearly all his strength to get to this point. Yet, as soon as he arrives, he suffers another humiliation. He is stripped of his clothes—he is left exposed, vulnerable.

Meditation

Most of us experience embarrassing moments, when we feel vulnerable, or open to attack, when we feel we have no defense. We wait for others' approval, and sometimes it doesn't come.

Being vulnerable is extremely difficult. It means standing up as you are, with nothing to cover up the blemishes, and asking others to accept you, warts and all.

Clothes, cars, and other material objects offer us a false sense of security. We can hide behind them. It is easier to be who you want to be with the right outfit or with a new car. Without these things, we feel we risk being rejected.

Reflection

Our worst fear is to have our inadequacies exposed to others in an unloving environment, especially when others' seem secure and protected.

Think about the last time you felt vulnerable or rejected. Maybe your embarrassment was caused by something as small as telling a joke that no one laughed at. Maybe you voiced something you believed in and everyone made fun of you.

Jesus is with us in our lonely and humiliating moments.

Pause for silent reflection.

Prayer

We pray to Jesus, our Lord, who suffered for us through humiliation and scorn.

Lord, grant us the open-mindedness to see past the inadequacies of ourselves and others so that we may unconditionally love and accept one another.

Eleventh Station

Jesus Is Nailed to the Cross

Think about the moment when our Lord is nailed to the cross. Left with only a strip of cloth around his hips, he must lie on top of the wood to have nails pierce his hands and feet so that his body can be made one with the wooden cross.

He is now one step away from death as the cross is raised. Everything possible has been done to destroy this man who is innocent of the crime with which he is charged. Only gravity can further persecute him.

Meditation

At one time or another, all of us have felt persecuted. We feel we are innocent and do not deserve the punishment that comes our way. When we feel as though we are victims of injustice, we experience a small fraction of what Jesus must have felt when the nails pierced his flesh. We wait for the nailing to cease; we pray for an end to our persecution.

All of us have also played the part of the persecutor—when we overindulge while persons in other parts of the world starve, when we take advantage of a friend's weakness for our own gain, or when we ignore wrongs that do not directly affect us. At these times, if we are honest with ourselves, we know that we will have to accept the consequences of our behavior.

Reflection

 Think about a time when you felt persecuted—when you felt as though you were the victim of injustice. Maybe you were the target of everyone's jokes, or maybe people just avoided you—refusing to talk to you—as a payback for something you didn't do.

Also think about a time when you have been the persecutor, when you have punished someone for something with which you found fault.

Pause for silent reflection.

Prayer

We pray to Jesus, our Lord, who was nailed to the cross of our sins.

Lord, help us endure the times when we are victims of injustice, and help us refrain from persecuting others.

Twelfth Station

Jesus Dies on the Cross

Think about the moment when our Lord dies on the cross. Darkness comes over the land at that hour, and Jesus cries out, "My God, my God, why have you forsaken me?" (Matthew 27:46) Before bowing his head to death, he utters, "Father, into your hands, I commend my spirit" (Luke 23:46).

The Gospels say that as our Lord breathes his last, the earth shakes, rocks are split, and tombs open. Many saints appear and gather near the holy body that hangs on the cross. When those keeping watch over Jesus see and hear the visions and earthquakes, they are filled with awe and exclaim, "Truly this man was God's Son!" (See Matthew 27:50-54.)

Meditation

Some of us have experienced the death of loved ones—grandparents, parents, siblings, or friends. We understand the turmoil that the Gospels describe. It feels as though life as we know it has ended, and we experience an inner earthquake—in which everything inside of us splits open and cracks.

It seems as though death is the final word, that there is nothing beyond it to give us hope. When we lose loved ones, it feels as though we have lost them forever, and we have no chance of ever relating to them, ever communicating with them, again.

Jesus tells and shows us otherwise. Death is not the last word. There is resurrection. The whole point of Jesus' death on the cross is to show us that death is conquered by love.

Reflection

Death is inevitable. Everyone who is born will eventually die. But death does not have to be final and hopeless. In Jesus' death comes an invitation to eternal life.

Think for a moment about a time in your life when you lost a relative or friend to death. Think also about those persons you've lost to divorce or to a separation of some sort—like a move to a new city. In your pain, remember that death and separation are not the last words. There is hope. There is everlasting life.

Pause for silent reflection.

Prayer

We pray to Jesus, our Lord and Savior, who lives on past his death.

Lord, by the mystery of your death and resurrection, we know life everlasting. Comfort us in our grieving and remind us of your promise of hope.

Thirteenth Station

Jesus Is Taken Down From the Cross

Think about the moment when our Lord is taken down from the cross. On the day before the Sabbath, a wealthy man from Arimathea asks Pilate for the body of Jesus. This man, Joseph, believes in the kingdom of God that Jesus described.

Joseph takes the body of Jesus down from the cross and lays it in a tomb where no one had ever been buried. Followers of Jesus wrap the body in linen cloths with a mixture of myrrh and aloes, as is the burial custom of the Jews.

Meditation

All of us are called to help our friends in different ways. Because of the unique talents, gifts, and resources each of us has, we can offer different things to persons in need. A friend with connections to a college may help us with our application for admission to that school. Another friend who is a good public speaker may serve as our campaign manager for a school election.

Just as the wise men in the nativity story bring unique offerings to the newly born Messiah, Joseph of Arimathea and other followers of Jesus contribute special gifts to the burial of Jesus' body.

After a humiliating death, Jesus is finally given the respect that is due him. Our Lord is given a proper burial, in keeping with the Jewish burial custom.

Reflection

 Think about a time when a friend, parent, or sibling did something especially kind for you, a generous act of love at a time you were sick or feeling down. A small sign of compassion can go a long way in a time of loneliness and depression.

Jesus encourages us to go out of our way to be loving and kind. Think about a person you know who is feeling down. How can you show your friend compassion?

Pause for silent reflection.

Prayer

We pray to Jesus, our Lord, who is always merciful and loving.

Lord, lead us in the ways of kindness and mercy. Teach us to be as loving and merciful to others as you are to us.

Fourteenth Station

Jesus Is Placed in the Tomb

hink about the moment when our Lord is placed in the tomb. Joseph of Arimathea, in his generosity and hospitality, lays the body of Jesus in a new tomb that he had cut out of rock. After the body is wrapped in linens and anointed with spices, Joseph rolls a stone against the entrance of the tomb.

Afraid that someone might steal the body and spread word that Jesus has risen, Pilate orders soldiers to secure the tomb by sealing the stone and by keeping watch there.

Next are the hours of anticipation and waiting before the sun rises on Easter.

Meditation

We hate waiting. Nothing is worse than sitting impatiently through the hours right before an important event. We glance at the clock every minute, and with every look, the second hand moves more and more slowly. It always seems at these moments that time is standing still, and that the hour we wait for will never arrive.

It is like this when Jesus is placed in the tomb. The turmoil and terror of the crucifixion are over, and everyone is anxious to see if the Lord will really rise on the third day as he said he would.

Skeptics suspect that one of Jesus' disciples will steal the body and say that he has risen. To ensure that this doesn't happen, Pilate takes all necessary precautions—sealing the rock at the entrance of the tomb and placing a guard there.

Pilate and his men, however, cannot stop what is to happen according to God. We know the end of the story. What Jesus said would happen does, in fact, come to pass. The hour the world is waiting for finally arrives, and anticipation and suspense turn to triumph and glory.

Reflection

Think about a time when you had to wait patiently for an answer, outcome, or result. Perhaps you waited to hear if you had made the team, had been accepted to a school, or had passed a difficult test. Perhaps you waited for news about a friend or relative or for an important phone call.

Remember the anxiety and restlessness that were part of the waiting. With Jesus' resurrection on Easter, the waiting comes to an end for believers.

Pause for silent reflection.

Prayer

We pray to Jesus, our Lord, whose resurrection put an end to our waiting.

Lord, grant us an end to our waiting. In our anxiety and restlessness, bring us the peace that comes in your name.